WHICH ????? ?
(DUDE)
ARE YOU?

PRICE STERN SLOAN
Published by the Penguin Group
Penguin Group (USA) LLC, 375 Hudson Street, New York, New York 10014, USA

USA | Canada | UK | Ireland | Australia | New Zealand | India | South Africa | China

penguin.com
A Penguin Random House Company

Published in 2015 by Price Stern Sloan, a division of Penguin Young Readers Group, 345 Hudson Street, New York, New York 10014. PSS! is a registered trademark of Penguin Group (USA) LLC. Printed in the USA.

ISBN 978-0-8431-8270-5   10 9 8 7 6 5 4 3 2 1

REGULAR SHOW

WHICH ????? (DUDE) ARE YOU?

BY KARL JONES

PSS!
Price Stern Sloan
An Imprint of Penguin Group (USA) LLC

TABLE OF CONTENTS

Hey, everyone, I'm Thomas. I'm an intern at the Park, and I guess that's why Benson asked me to introduce this cool quiz book about all the different bros that appear on REGULAR SHOW. I asked him if I was going to get paid overtime to work on the project, and he just glared at me and screamed, "THOMAS!"

I guess that's a no.

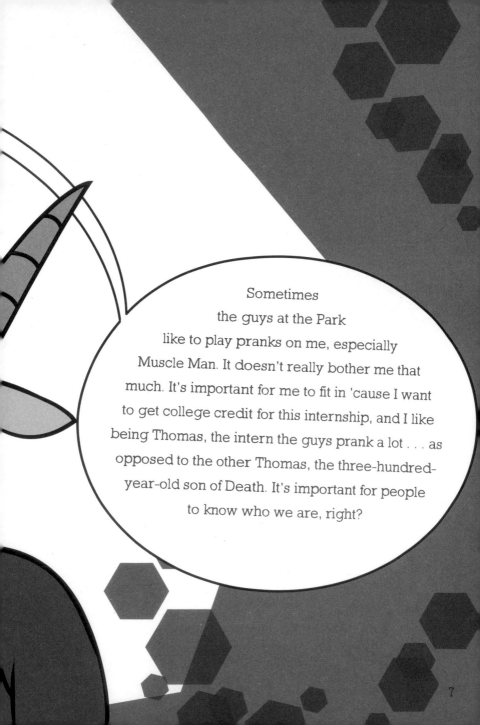

Sometimes the guys at the Park like to play pranks on me, especially Muscle Man. It doesn't really bother me that much. It's important for me to fit in 'cause I want to get college credit for this internship, and I like being Thomas, the intern the guys prank a lot . . . as opposed to the other Thomas, the three-hundred-year-old son of Death. It's important for people to know who we are, right?

WHICH THOMAS ARE YOU?

There are two Thomases on **REGULAR SHOW**. One is a happy intern who works at the Park, and the other is the three-hundred-year-old son of Death. Want to find out which Thomas you are most like? Answer the questions and add up your score to find out.

1. What's your preferred article of clothing?

A. Periwinkle footie pajamas

B. Gray T-shirt and khaki pants

2. If asked, what would your friends be more likely to call you?

A. A goat intern

B. A demon baby

3. Which would you rather pretend?

A. You are actually only eight months old.

B. You're only doing an internship at the Park for college credit.

4. What would you rather do for entertainment?

A. Tell a bad scary story

B. Read baby books

5. **Which one of these is more likely to be your mom?**

    A. Death's wife

    B. A nice lady who likes talking on a cell phone

6. **What are you more likely to do on a Saturday night?**

    A. Go to an awesome costume party with your friends from the Park

    B. Be babysat by Mordecai and Rigby

7. **Who is more likely to yell at you?**

    A. Death

    B. Benson

8. **Which of these is closer to your actual age?**

    A. Twentysomething

    B. Three hundred years old

Now, add up the number of a answers to the odd-numbered questions (1, 3, 5, 7). Add up the number of b answers to the even-numbered questions (2, 4, 6, 8). Add these two numbers together. If the total is four or less, then you're Thomas the Park intern. If the total is more than four, then you're Thomas the son of Death.

MORDECAI

◇ Likes to make up raps with his best friend, Rigby

◇ Is a total slacker

◇ Is the lead singer of the band Mordecai and the Rigbys

◇ Is dating CJ

◇ Loves drinking joe with his bro

IDENTITY CRISIS

When Garrett Bobby Ferguson Jr. takes over the Park and builds a huge freeway exit called Exit 9B, everyone but Mordecai and Rigby get brainwashed and go to work on other jobs. Draw lines to match the **REGULAR SHOW** characters with their brainwashed occupations.

Construction Manager

Butterfly Caretaker

Mechanic

Quantum Physics Professor

Pizza Delivery Guy

Mordecai and Rigby have traveled two months into the future and must find a way to trigger the memories of their friends so they can sign the petition and take back the Park from Garrett Bobby Ferguson Jr. Match the memory that brings each of their friends back to reality.

Only Woman He Ever Loved

Lollipop

"MY MOM" Joke

A High Five

DO YOU KNOW THIS BRO?:

BENSON

- ⬡ Can play the most difficult drum solo of all time

- ⬡ Is the manager of the Park

- ⬡ Loves yelling at Mordecai and Rigby

- ⬡ Face turns bright red when he gets mad

- ⬡ His boss is Mr. Maellard

REGULAR SHOW
CATCHPHRASES

At first, Mordecai and Rigby aren't able to get Benson's memory back, and he is fighting on Garrett Bobby Ferguson Jr.'s side. He is about to destroy Mordo and Rigs when they are finally able to jog his memory by saying which of these classic REGULAR SHOW catchphrases?

Woooooooooooo!

Yeah-yuh!

Hambonin'!

Punchies

15

ROCK-PAPER-SCISSORS!

NAME: _____

FRIEND'S NAME:
_____

Back in Lolliland, we call this game "quartz-parchment-shears."

WIN / LOSE / TIE

Rock beats scissors.
Scissors beats paper. Paper beats rock.
Mordecai and Rigby love to play rock-paper-scissors, even though Benson says it's an evil game. The two best friends are always keeping track of who has won more often. Play rock-paper-scissors with your best friend and keep track of how many times you win, lose, or tie in the spaces below. Add up your scores at the end.

NAME:_____

FRIEND'S NAME:

_____

WIN / LOSE / TIE

NAME:_____

FRIEND'S NAME:
_____

WIN / LOSE / TIE

It's an evil game!

I wonder who is best at "quartz-parchment-shears"?

NAME:_____

FRIEND'S NAME: _____

WIN / LOSE / TIE

Add up your scores to see who won the most rounds. High fives all around!

FINAL SCORE _____

DO YOU KNOW THIS BRO?: RIGBY

- ⬡ Loves slacking off

- ⬡ Loves playing video games with his best friend, Mordecai

- ⬡ Thinks Eileen is kind of annoying

- ⬡ Has a brother named Don, who he also finds annoying

- ⬡ Loves hambonin'

WHICH DUDE IS THIS?:

PART ONE

These are a bunch of characters that you might recognize from different episodes. Write their names in the blanks. If you're having trouble remembering, check the hints!

Hint: Rock-paper-scissors

_____

Hint: Hot-dog competition

_____

Hint: Mommy Monthly

Hint: Video Game Monthly

Hint:
"You happened!"

Hint: Fists of Justice

Hint: Ulti-Meatum

Hint: Confused knight

_____

Hint: Her son is
three hundred
years old!

Hint: Messenger for
the Guardians of
Eternal Youth

Hint: His light-up
tie wasn't cheap.

_____

_____

Hint: Hi-Five's
brother

Hint: They
wanted Muscle
Man to be a pregnant
stomach model.

_____

Hint: East Pines

_____

Hint: They live in
the Park fountain.

DO YOU KNOW THIS BRO?:

SKIPS

- ⬡ Used to be called Walks

- ⬡ Vowed to skip ever since he lost the love of his life

- ⬡ Is a yeti

- ⬡ Has to perform the Spirit Dance every year to maintain his immortality

- ⬡ Had to battle his own stress monster

EVERYONE LOVES DON!

1. TRUE OR FALSE: Don is Rigby's older brother.

2. When Don asks for you to give him some sugar, it means
A. He likes his coffee sweet.
B. He needs sugar for a baking recipe.
C. He wants to give you a hug.
D. He works at a supermarket, and they have run out of sugar.

4. Don drives a
A. Golf cart
B. Minivan
C. Tank
D. Corvette

3. TRUE OR FALSE: Even though he is younger, Don is taller than Rigby.

5. TRUE OR FALSE:

Don is an accountant who helps the Park with an audit.

6. How long has Rigby hated Don?

A. Since his sixth birthday when Don stole the attention of his friends

B. Since Don hugged Rigby in front of a girl he liked

C. Since Don showed up at the Park to help with the audit

D. All his life

7. TRUE OR FALSE:

Don is allergic to peanuts.

8. Don thinks Rigby is

A. Annoying

B. Intelligent

C. Cool

D. Skinny

MATCHMAKER, MATCHMAKER!

If you were a guy on REGULAR SHOW, which character would you end up dating? Take this quiz to find the answer.

1. What's your favorite thing to do on a date?

A. Slow dance after everyone leaves the party

B. Play mini golf

C. Have a fancy dinner at a bistro

D. Explode submarines

2. Whom would you be most likely to talk to at a party?

A. A tall, friendly robin

B. A shy, intelligent mole

C. A large, passionate green woman

D. A cloud humanoid

3. Which of these attributes would you want your girlfriend to possess?

A. Kind-hearted, caring, and down-to-earth

B. Intelligent and willing to correct people when they're wrong

C. Demanding and passionate

D. Witty and independent

4. Your girlfriend is most likely to wear which of the following?

A. Jeans and yellow shirts
B. Hoodies
C. A skirt and a T-shirt
D. A striped tank top

5. What would you guys talk about on your date?

A. One of your favorite bands, Fist Pump
B. The proper way to do a pull-up
C. That time you went to the prom together
D. Dodgeball

6. What's your favorite hair color?

A. Red
B. Brown
C. Olive green
D. Pure white

7. Your girlfriend is most likely to enjoy which of the following?

A. Hanging out with family and friends at a BBQ

B. Chiming in to your made-up rap song with unfunny facts

C. Kissing her boyfriend

D. "Burning" you

8. What would you be most afraid of your girlfriend finding out?

A. That you asked her out because of a bet

B. That you think she's good at starting fires

C. That you have a bald spot

D. That you gave movie tickets to another girl

Add up your A, B, C, and D scores. If you have mostly As, then your best match is Margaret. If mostly Bs, you'd be best matched with Eileen. If you answered mostly C, your girlfriend should definitely be Starla. If you answered mostly D, your girlfriend should be CJ.

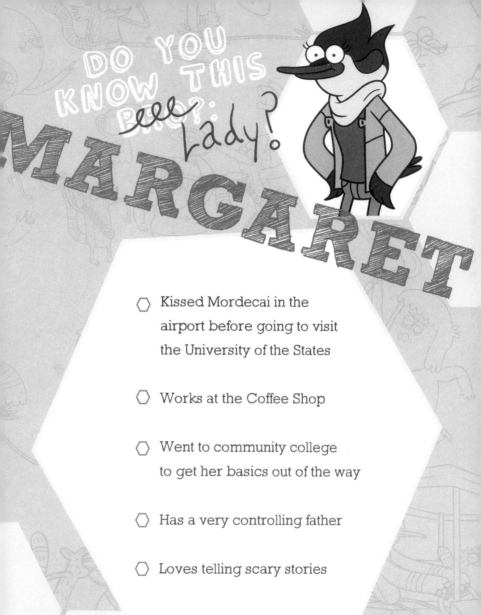

DO YOU KNOW THIS BRO?: Lady?

MARGARET

○ Kissed Mordecai in the airport before going to visit the University of the States

○ Works at the Coffee Shop

○ Went to community college to get her basics out of the way

○ Has a very controlling father

○ Loves telling scary stories

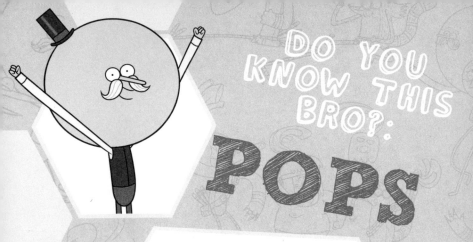

DO YOU KNOW THIS BRO?: POPS

⬡ Loves his subscription to *Moustaches Monthly*

⬡ Is originally from Lolliland

⬡ Loves to play quartz-parchment-shears

⬡ Is Mr. Maellard's son

⬡ Is very fancy

⬡ Loves his creepy doll

TRAILER VERSUS HOME

Most of the bros at the Park live in Muscle Man's trailer or Pops's home. Out of the two, which one are you more familiar with? Read the list of objects below and try to guess if they come from Muscle Man's trailer or Pops's home.

1. A faded pink sofa
A. Muscle Man's trailer
B. Pops's home

2. An office used by Benson and Mr. Maellard
A. Muscle Man's trailer
B. Pops's home

3. A trampoline
A. Muscle Man's trailer
B. Pops's home

4. A Dark Side of the Moon poster
A. Muscle Man's trailer
B. Pops's home

5. A room with nothing but a box and a closet

A. Muscle Man's trailer

B. Pops's home

6. A computer sign-up sheet

A. Muscle Man's trailer

B. Pops's home

7. Lots of trash and clothes on the floor

A. Muscle Man's trailer

B. Pops's home

8. A dirty attic

A. Muscle Man's trailer

B. Pops's home

9. A broken TV

A. Muscle Man's trailer

B. Pops's home

10. A file cabinet

A. Muscle Man's trailer

B. Pops's home

DO YOU KNOW THIS BRO?:
MUSCLE MAN

- ○ Won his trailer in a hot-dog-eating contest

- ○ Loves his girlfriend, Starla, so much he would eat wheat germ for her

- ○ His real name is Mitch Sorenstein

- ○ Loves to make "MY MOM" jokes

- ○ Loves flexing his pecs

HI-FIVE GHOST

- ⬡ Is Muscle Man's best friend

- ⬡ Gives the best high fives

- ⬡ Is known for his driving skills

- ⬡ Is also known as Fives, HFG, and Hi-Five

- ⬡ Likes Downtempo Electronica

1. "Okay, men, this is the hour of our prominence. On my signal, charge!"

2. "Fellas, I've been around the block a few times. There's something evil in that computer; we gotta smash it."

3. "She must think I'm a total loser!"

I always try to pay attention to what other people are saying. Like I said, I have to get college credit for this.

37

4. "Dude, forget it! You wanna order a measly two-egg breakfast, that's fine by me. But when you finish and you're still hungry, don't come crying to me, 'cause I ain't sharin'."

5. "Can you guys stop making me laugh? It hurts when I smile."

6. "Congratulations, you've figured it out. You're the first gamers to realize that hanging out with your friends is more important than a stupid glove."

7. "Hey, guys. Here's your coffee."

8. "Ooh, I want my Ulti-Meatum Idaho-style!"

9. "So, what do you say? How would you like a job at the Park?"

10. "I'd like to change my name back!"

11. "Mordecai, Rigby—
we can all be turds!"

12. "Mordecai and the Rigbys?
What happened to Mustache
Cash Stash?"

13. "'Ello, Gov'nor!"

That movie
looks scary!

DO YOU KNOW THIS ~~BRO?~~ Lady?

EILEEN

⬡ Raps about thermonuclear fusion

⬡ Is a really cute mole

⬡ Works at the Coffee Shop

⬡ Loves science

⬡ Is great at starting fires

DRAWSOME!

**This game is called Drawsome, because you draw and it's ...
AWESOME! Here's how you play:**

1. Call your friends and tell them to come over because it's DRAWSOME TIME!

2. Take a small piece of paper and write down a noun. This could be a person, a place, or a thing. That's what the word **noun** means. Zingo!

3. Fold it up and don't show it to anyone.

4. Have a friend time you for thirty seconds while you begin drawing what you wrote on the piece of paper from step #2. You can draw on the opposite page.

5. Your friends have to guess what you're drawing, so make sure you draw really awesomely. Use these next few pages to play!

You guys ready for some Drawsome?

Wait, I have a joke first.

I say, "Ask me if I'm a tree."

Then you say, "Are you a tree?"

Then I say, "No?"

(silence)

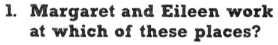

AWESOME LADIES!

1. Margaret and Eileen work at which of these places?

A. The Coffee Shop

B. The Café

C. The Restaurant

D. Taco Tim's Salsa Emporium

2. TRUE OR FALSE:

CJ is an excellent dodgeball player.

3. Margaret and Mordecai were trapped in the Friend Zone because . . . ?

A. The asteroid didn't like them.

B. There was a trap set for them on the mountain.

C. Mordecai waited too long to kiss Margaret.

D. They didn't get out of the car fast enough.

4. TRUE OR FALSE:

The *C* in CJ stands for corny.

5. Mordecai, Rigby, Margaret, and Eileen were once attacked by which of these forest creatures?

A. Marsh Dude

B. Stag-Man

C. Jean, the Very Bossy Sparrow

D. Ms. Tree

6. TRUE OR FALSE:

Eileen is allergic to "horse wind."

47

7. What is Margaret's last name?

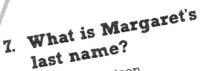

A. Margaretson

B. Bodnar

C. Quetzalcoatl

D. Smith

8. Mordecai and Margaret have been to which of these locations?

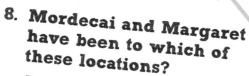

A. Kissyface Point

B. Cuddle Cul-de-sac

C. Snug Harbor

D. Make-Out Mountain

WHICH DUDE IS THIS?: PART TWO

In the blank spaces, write the names of the different characters shown below. If you're having trouble remembering, check the hints!

Hint: He's a cyborg.

_____

Hint: They took a plane to get to the Park to see Mordecai.

_____

Hint: More uptight than Benson

_____

Hint: He's a claustrophobic yeti.

_____

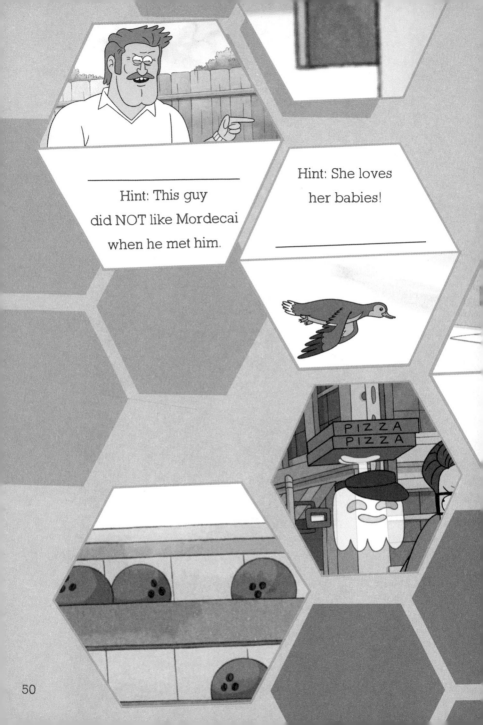

Hint: This guy did NOT like Mordecai when he met him.

Hint: She loves her babies!

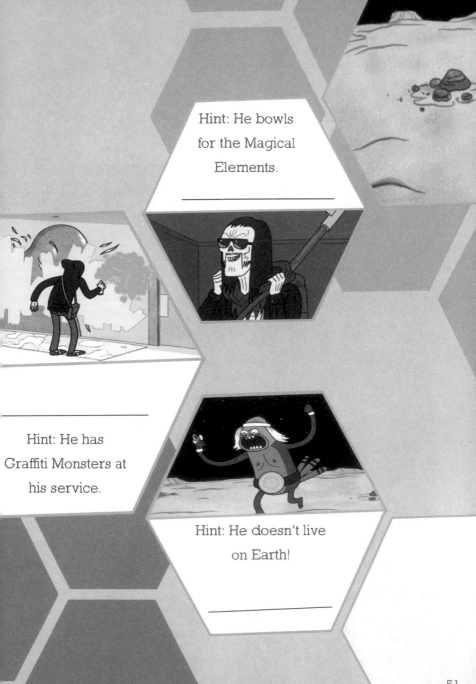

Hint: He bowls for the Magical Elements.

_____

Hint: He has Graffiti Monsters at his service.

Hint: He doesn't live on Earth!

_____

Hint: They're the opposite of Mordecai and Rigby . . . sort of.

_____

Hint: He lives in a cave.

Hint: She will disappear when everyone reveals secrets with deep meaning.

_____

_____

Hint: She was hired to replace Benson.

DO YOU KNOW THIS Beeee... Lady?

STARLA

- ⬡ Is Muscle Man's awesome girlfriend

- ⬡ Is the only person that calls him by his real name

- ⬡ Has green skin, just like Muscle Man

- ⬡ Loves to smooch her man!

WHO ARE YOU?!

1. **Which of the following best describes your personality?**
   A. I follow the beat of my own hambonin'!
   B. My friends are important, and I look out for them.
   C. Stressed? Of course I'm stressed!
   D. I don't sweat the small stuff.
   E. I'm sweet like a licorice stick.
   F. I don't know. Why don't you ask MY MOM!

2. **What kinds of books do you like?**
   A. Adventure!
   B. Joke books
   C. Books about park management
   D. I'm partial to biographies.
   E. Oooooh, I like comic books!
   F. Anything about MY MOM!

3. **If you could take a road trip anywhere on Earth, where would you go?**
   A. Aw, man. Why does it have to be on Earth? What about space?!
   B. Meteor Mountain would be a cool place.
   C. Do you think I have time for road trips?
   D. Some place nice and simple.
   E. Oh my! I love road trips!
   F. MY MOM's house!

4. What is your perfect day?

A. Wake up. Get into trouble.

B. Have some coffee. Help my friend get out of trouble.

C. Everyone does exactly what I tell them to!

D. Handle whatever comes my way.

E. Reading my copy of *Moustaches Monthly*!

F. A date with Starla and . . . call MY MOM.

Wow. These questions are heavy. Time to get serious . . .

5. If you were in a band, what would your role be?

A. Lead guitar!

B. Front man, lead vocals

C. Well, I don't have time to be in a band, but I'd play the drums.

D. I'll be security.

E. I can play the triangle.

F. I'd be a solo act called MY MOM.

6. What's one of your biggest talents?

A. Hambonin'!

B. Donuts!

C. Responsibility

D. Super strength

E. Turning a quick phrase

F. MY MOM says I'm lazy.

7. When you encounter a giant monster, how do you react?

A. Run away and get help!

B. Try not to run away.

C. Yell!

D. Fight it.

E. I'm scared just thinking about it!

F. Ask MY MOM what to do.

8. When you are playing Drawsome, is winning a priority?

A. Winning is awesome! Losing is for losers.

B. Winning is cool, but I like hanging with my bros.

C. I don't have time for Drawsome.

D. It's how you play the game that matters.

E. Ooooh, can we play quartz-parchment-shears next?

F. If I win something I'd give it to MY MOM.

I wish I knew who I was . . .

. . . just kidding!

YOU ARE . . .

If you answered A to most of the questions, you are RIGBY! You're a fly-by-the-seat-of-your-pants kind of guy who loves adventure, even though it often gets you into trouble.

If you answered B to most of the questions, you are MORDECAI! You love to chill out and relax. Your friends are really important to you, and they look to you for guidance and support.

If you answered C to most of the questions, you are BENSON! You're focused and driven. Sometimes a little too much! It wouldn't hurt you to loosen up a little.

If you answered D to most of the questions, you are SKIPS! You're peaceful and calm. You try not to let other people's drama affect you, but when it does, you're always there to help.

If you answered E to most of the questions, you are POPS! You live in a magical dreamworld filled with candy, happiness, and little baby bunnies hopping on your belly.

If you answered F to most of the questions, you are MUSCLE MAN! You're a weirdo who is obsessed with his own mother. You should seek professional help before it's too late.

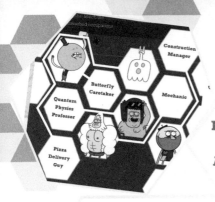

IDENTITY CRISIS ANSWERS

REGULAR SHOW CATCHPHRASES

Wooooooooooo! correct
Yeah-yuh! nope
Hambonin'! correct
Punchies nope
Whoooooaaaaaa! correct
Joe with my bro nope
Hmm-mmm. Hmm. Hmm. correct
Not setting up the chairs next time! *Not setting
up the chairs next time!* correct

WHICH DUDE IS THIS?: PART ONE ANSWERS

Frank Jones
  Hint: Hot-dog competition
Rauchambeau Monster
  Hint: Rock-paper-scissors
Dante
  Hint: *Video Game Monthly*
Muscle Man
  Hint: *Mommy Monthly*
The Urge
  Hint: "You happened!"
Klorgbane the Destroyer
  Hint: Fists of Justice
Ajay Moldinado
  Hint: Ulti-Meatum
Sir Gabelthorpe
  Hint: Confused knight

Death's wife
  Hint: Her son is
  three hundred years old!
Gary
  Hint: Messenger for the Guardians
  of Eternal Youth
Uncle Steve
  Hint: His light-up tie wasn't cheap
Lo-Five Ghost
  Hint: Hi-Five's brother
Filbert and Mulligan
  Hint: They wanted Muscle Man to
  be a pregnant stomach model.
Gene
  Hint: East Pines
Baby Ducks
  Hint: They live in the Park fountain.

Everyone Loves Don!
ANSWERS

1. TRUE OR FALSE: Don is Rigby's older brother.

   FALSE

2. When Don asks for you to give him some sugar, it means

   C. He wants to give you a hug.

3. TRUE OR FALSE: Even though he is younger, Don is taller than Rigby.

   TRUE

4. Don drives a

   D. Corvette

5. TRUE OR FALSE: Don is an accountant who helps the Park with an audit.

   TRUE

6. How long has Rigby hated Don?

   A. Since his sixth birthday when Don stole the attention of his friends.

7. TRUE OR FALSE: Don is allergic to peanuts.

   FALSE

8. Don thinks Rigby is

   C. Cool

TRAILER VERSUS HOME ANSWERS

1. A faded pink sofa
   A. Muscle Man's trailer

2. An office used by Benson and Mr. Maellard
   B. Pops's home

3. A trampoline
   B. Pops's home

4. A Dark Side of the Moon poster
   A. Muscle Man's trailer

5. A room with nothing but a box and a closet
   B. Pops's home

6. A computer sign-up sheet
   B. Pops's home

7. Lots of trash and clothes on the floor
   A. Muscle Man's trailer

8. A dirty attic
   B. Pops's home

9. A broken TV
   A. Muscle Man's trailer

10. A file cabinet
    B. Pops's home

1. "Okay, men, this is the hour of our prominence. On my signal, charge!" answer: Pops

2. "Fellas, I've been around the block a few times. There's something evil in that computer; we gotta smash it." answer: Skips

3. "She must think I'm a total loser!" answer: Mordecai

4. "Dude, forget it! You wanna order a measly two-egg breakfast, that's fine by me. But when you finish and you're still hungry, don't come crying to me, 'cause I ain't sharin'." answer: Rigby

5. "Can you guys stop making me laugh? It hurts when I smile." answer: Muscle Man

6. "Congratulations, you've figured it out. You're the first gamers to realize that hanging out with your friends is more important than a stupid glove." answer: Giant Maximum Glove

7. "Hey, guys. Here's your coffee." answer: Eileen

8. "Ooh, I want my Ulti-Meatum Idaho-style!" answer: Pops

9. "So, what do you say? How would you like a job at the Park?" answer: Benson

10. "I'd like to change my name back!" answer: Rigby

11. "Mordecai, Rigby—we can all be turds!" answer: Pops

12. "Mordecai and the Rigbys? What happened to Mustache Cash Stash?" answer: Mordecai

13. "'Ello, Gov'nor!" answer: British Taxi

1. Margaret and Eileen work at which of these places?

   A. The Coffee Shop

2. TRUE OR FALSE: CJ is an excellent dodgeball player.

   True

3. Margaret and Mordecai were trapped in the Friend Zone because . . . ?

   C. Mordecai waited too long to kiss Margaret.

4. TRUE OR FALSE: The C in CJ stands for corny.

   False

5. Mordecai, Rigby, Margaret, and Eileen were once attacked by which of these forest creatures?

   B. Stag-Man

6. TRUE OR FALSE: Eileen is allergic to "horse wind."

   False

7. What is Margaret's last name?

   D. Smith

8. Mordecai and Margaret have been to which of these locations?

   D. Make-Out Mountain

Techmo

Hint: He's a cyborg.

Mordecai's parents

Hint: They took a plane to get to the Park to see Mordecai.

Quips

Hint: He's a claustrophobic yeti.

Headmaster Bennett

Hint: More uptight than Benson.

Frank Smith/Margaret's father

Hint: This guy did NOT like Mordecai when he met him.

Mother Duck

Hint: She loves her babies!

Death

Hint: He bowls for the Magical Elements.

Park Avenue

Hint: He has Graffiti Monsters at his service.

Moon Monster

Hint: He doesn't live on Earth!

Yacedrom & Ygbyr

Hint: They're the opposite of Mordecai and Rigby . . . sort of.

Death Bear

Hint: He lives in a cave.

Guardian of Secrets

Hint: She will disappear when everyone reveals secrets with deep meaning.

Susan

Hint: She was hired to replace Benson.

FINAL SCORE

Add up all your correct answers!

100+ Points
You are a
TECHNOMANCER!

80+ Points
You are a
WARRIOR KNIGHT!

70+ Points
You are a
PIRATE SAMURAI!

60+ Points
You are a
VAMPIRE-ARCHER!

50+ Points
You are a
CYBORG COWBOY!

Fewer than
50 Points
Time to watch more
REGULAR SHOW!
Yeah-yuh!

Well, I have to say I've learned a lot in my internship at the Park, and I hope you've learned a lot from this book. But, I just lost another bet with Muscle Man, so now I have to go put this pizza costume back on until the end of the world!